YOUR KNOWLEDGE HAS VALUE

- We will publish your bachelor's and master's thesis, essays and papers

- Your own eBook and book - sold worldwide in all relevant shops

- Earn money with each sale

Upload your text at www.GRIN.com and publish for free

Anna Lena Bischoff

Advertisement reading. The hidden message in marketing

GRIN Verlag

Bibliografische Information der Deutschen Nationalbibliothek:

Die Deutsche Bibliothek verzeichnet diese Publikation in der Deutschen National-
bibliografie; detaillierte bibliografische Daten sind im Internet über http://dnb.d-
nb.de/ abrufbar.

Imprint:

Copyright © 2011 GRIN Verlag GmbH
Druck und Bindung: Books on Demand GmbH, Norderstedt Germany
ISBN: 978-3-656-76590-5

This book at GRIN:

http://www.grin.com/en/e-book/282296/advertisement-reading-the-hidden-message-
in-marketing

GRIN - Your knowledge has value

Der GRIN Verlag publiziert seit 1998 wissenschaftliche Arbeiten von Studenten, Hochschullehrern und anderen Akademikern als eBook und gedrucktes Buch. Die Verlagswebsite www.grin.com ist die ideale Plattform zur Veröffentlichung von Hausarbeiten, Abschlussarbeiten, wissenschaftlichen Aufsätzen, Dissertationen und Fachbüchern.

Visit us on the internet:

http://www.grin.com/

http://www.facebook.com/grincom

http://www.twitter.com/grin_com

This add is taken out of the spring issue of Vogue magazine in 2008. It features a photography showing an elderly man sitting in a limousine, driving through Berlin with a patterned travelling bag besides him. The caption says "a journey brings us face to face with ourselves". Looking more closely one notices the add presents a Louis Vuitton bag. Furthermore is the man not an ordinary person, but Mikhail Gorbachev, a former governor of the Soviet Union. Him driving through Berlin describes a much more denotative picture.

The advertisement is a centerfold piece, which can be divided into three vertical columns.

The first and last column are backround, whereas the second column is filled by Gorbachevs figure.The Berlin Wall is placed horizontally in the backround and runs parallel with the bag. The window frames of the car are running from the left and right side towards Gorbachev's face. Through that attention is drawn to his face as his head forms the center corner of the window frames. It seems as if the face is illuminated by the collar of his shirt.

The car is spacious and old in an antique way and radiates comfort and nostalgia.

The add has a very calm atmosphere to it as if everything hectic is not able to enter the car the reader is within.

The colours used for the car interior and Gorbachevs clothes are rather dark with the exceptions of his face and hands, windows and the actual bag.

The first thing the viewer looks at is Gorbachev's hand in the middle of the picture. One then moves up to his face where one follows his gaze outside the window in the distance and it is then when one notices the Berlin Wall. Gorbachevs left hand is resting on the doorhandle of the car. The grey fog throughout the picture makes the situation seem very forlorn and dismal. Gorbachev gazes thoughtfully in the distance. He appears to be tired and fragile.

The viewer then wanders to the right side in search for something more to add to the advertisement. The actual product to be sold is not in the focus of the add and gets noticed by the reader rather late. Nevertheless it is proven that adds to the right hand side get recognized more than ones on the left hand side. Therefore the bag is placed purposely. Moreover it is not clear whether the bag is part of the backround or foreground. Compared to Gorbachev, the bag is quite big, though. The bag and Gorbachev are placed at the same height and are both "sitting" on the same bench. Therefore the bag and Gorbachev are equalized in importance. The bag is closely snuggling up to Gorbachev and in consideration of the size of it, it almost seems like a puppy. This also fits with the time traveling analogy. A dog can be a trusty, lifelong friend that follows its owner everywhere. The product gets personified and adds a personal touch to the picture.

If one didn't know better, one would think that the picture got taken during the time when the Berlin Wall still existed. There is nothing in the add that depicts a reference to nowadays except for the Louis Vuitton bag and a magazine peeking out of it.

However the advertisement has been set in such an historic backround it clearly envisions nowadays. The setting is considered to be a historic moment which it wouldn't have been a while ago. Enough time has passed to envision symbols as the Berlin Wall as turning points in history rather than recent history. As Goldman stated, this is a unification of present and past.

The reference of Gorbachev and the Berlin Wall implicates change and the beginning of a new era. The add doesn't show any barbed wire or border patrol. There is nothing threatening in this picture as it has been when the GDR still existed.

Furthermore is the magazine peeking out of the bag referring to a very recent topic. The murder of Alexander Litvinenko. It says "The Murder of Litvinenko: They Wanted to Give Up the Suspect for $7,000."

The caption is written in a clear font without any frills. There is no verbs in it which makes it less emotional and more manly. Furthermore the "us" makes the reader part of a certain "in-crowd". The sentence has several meanings. Firs of all it might simply describe that travelling with a Louis Vuitton bag let's you discover new features about yourself. But it also hints at Gorbachevs history and his involvement of the fall of the Berlin wall. His own journey in regards to his struggle with himself to find his own place. By western countries, he was seen as one of the leading keyfigures to putting the cold war to an end non aggressively and fueling the Glasnost (openness) and Perestroika (restructuring) for which he received the Nobel Peace Prize. On the other hand he was regarded as weak and uncharismatic by former Soviet Union countries as he was not able to avoid the break and failure of the Soviet Union and caused political instability. Thus this picture shows his inner conflict as a "western" politician, carrying a bag that stands for luxury, wealth and the western lifestyle, in an "eastern" surrounding that has no longer something to offer for him as it is dull and depressing. It is as if he is moving on to some greater place, leaving the bitterness behind him.

Notably the bag is the only item in the add that has a little brighter color to it. The bag glorifies that somewhere along the way there will be something better out there. By carrying this bag the reader will be able to reach out to their own, westernized destination across the Berlin wall overcoming their shadows of the past.

All this is underlined by the use of light. It is much more bright outside the car than it is inside the limousine. With a Louis Vuitton bag one will be travelling to the bright side of life.

It also tells the reader that they can make a difference by carrying such a bag. They will be considered as significant and classy. It has a time travelling vibe to it as if to say by wearing this bag now you will be more important in several years and your bag will be your timeless time capsule.

The add aims at people who are aware of the historic back round and do know who Gorbachev is. Thus people who have been at least teens around 1989. Louis Vuitton also refers to its roots as a luggage selling company and not an luxury selling empire. This is implicated by a man having a travelling bag with him as opposed to a woman carrying a handbag. The reader of the add feels taken seriously as the add is captures a severe historical moment and not a garish bright cloud of color and refers to a well respected public figure.

In general the add doesn't use the typical features of advertisement. There is no pretty, happy famous figure praising a new product in a bright and colorful backround. Using politicians in adds is very controversial and risky. I assume that the add would not have been successful in countries of the former Soviet Union.

Finally it is an advert that is very different from the majority of the adds that have been published recently. It is not trying to draw a perfect picture. It much more gains attention by its controversial approach and by being different. The deeper meaning it carries along might be distasteful. Using the political backround of the cold war leaves a certain staleness to the picture. It is questionable whether it is ethically correct to turn a bag into a political object and to use it as historic time machine. Or to even compare wearing the "right" bag with a inflection point in history. Nevertheless makes it people stop and think and has a deeper meaning to it than so many other adds.

3